FOOD EXPERIMENTS
for Would-Be Scientists

Food Book for Children

Children's Science & Nature Books

BABY PROFESSOR
EDUCATION KIDS

Speedy Publishing LLC
40 E. Main St. #1156
Newark, DE 19711
www.speedypublishing.com

In this book, we're going to cover some fun food experiments. So, let's get right to it!

When you work in the kitchen, there are lots of ingredients you can mix up that will give you chemical reactions. Make sure your parents or another responsible adult are there in your *"lab"* with you.

Playful fun time in kitchen with kids.

Popping candy.

EXPERIMENTING WITH CANDY POPS

What You'll Need: Popping candy, some medium-sized bowls, some oil like vegetable oil, water, vinegar, and other ingredients you may want to try.

What You'll Do: Open up the popping candy and put a small quantity in each bowl. Add vinegar to one, water to the next one, and oil to the third.

What You'll Observe: The candy fizzes really fast in the vinegar and bubbles up. It fizzes in water too, but it's faster in the vinegar. In the oil, nothing happens.

The Science Behind It: Popping candy is manufactured by heating all the ingredients and then trapping carbon dioxide, in gas form, into it. These tiny bubbles of CO_2 are trapped inside the candy and what ultimately make it pop. It's a lot of fun to eat it because it bubbles and pops in your mouth when it reacts with your saliva.

Things To Think About: Why do you think the candy fizzes faster in vinegar than in water? What does your answer tell you about your saliva?

Colorful popping candy in a glass.

Whole block butter on a wooden background.

MAKING BUTTER

What You'll Need: Heavy whipping cream, a container with a tight-fitting lid like a mason jar.

What You'll Do: Let the cream warm to the temperature of the room. Pour the cream into the container about halfway and then shut the lid tight. Shake the jar until you feel something forming. You might have to shake a lot, but it's fun!

What You'll Observe: Your cream should have turned into a lump of butter with some liquid that looks kind of milky around its edges. It's safe for you to taste your homemade butter. What do you think of its taste? Remember that butter you buy in the store has flavor and preservatives added to it.

Cream in wooden bowl.

The Science Behind It: Cream and butter are both substances that are colloids. Types of colloids include gels, sols, and emulsions. The particles in these substances don't settle, and they can't be separated by ordinary filtering. All this means is that when you shake the cream the particles of fat stick together, and that, with enough shaking, forms butter! Now you know how butter becomes butter in a hand-cranked butter churner.

Things To Think About: How do you think butter was first discovered? Can you do some research online and find out?

Butter

Milk

GLUE FROM MILK

What You'll Need: A strainer like you use for spaghetti, a pan, some water, some milk, white vinegar, baking soda.

What You'll Do: Put a pan on the stove and heat up about 1 $^{1/2}$ cups of milk. Once the milk starts forming bubbles around the edges, then add about 3 teaspoons of vinegar. Keep heating and stirring until it starts to change.

You'll soon see some solid parts forming and some liquid parts separating away from the solid parts. The solid parts are called curd and the liquid part is called whey. Strain the mixture carefully through your sieve. You'll have solid lumps that look something like cottage cheese.

White vinegar in glass vial over wooden background.

Put the clumpy mixture back in the pan and add just a bit of water and about a tablespoon of baking soda. Heat up the mixture until it's bubbling. Then stir for a while and turn off the heat. Time to let your new glue cool so you can use it. You might need to add a bit more water or baking soda until you get a consistency that's like the thick paste glue that you use in school.

Once it's completely cooled you can try gluing some things together with it. Be careful though, because it works and there's no way to un-glue it!

What You'll Observe: Mixed with the other ingredients, your milk went through some changes. It first changed to curds and whey. Then, it became a paste.

The Science Behind It: The curds you formed are a milk protein that's called casein, which happens to be a natural glue.

Things To Think About: Do you think commercial glue is made this way? Why or why not?

Baking soda in bottle and wooden spoon.

Kid playing with hand made goo.

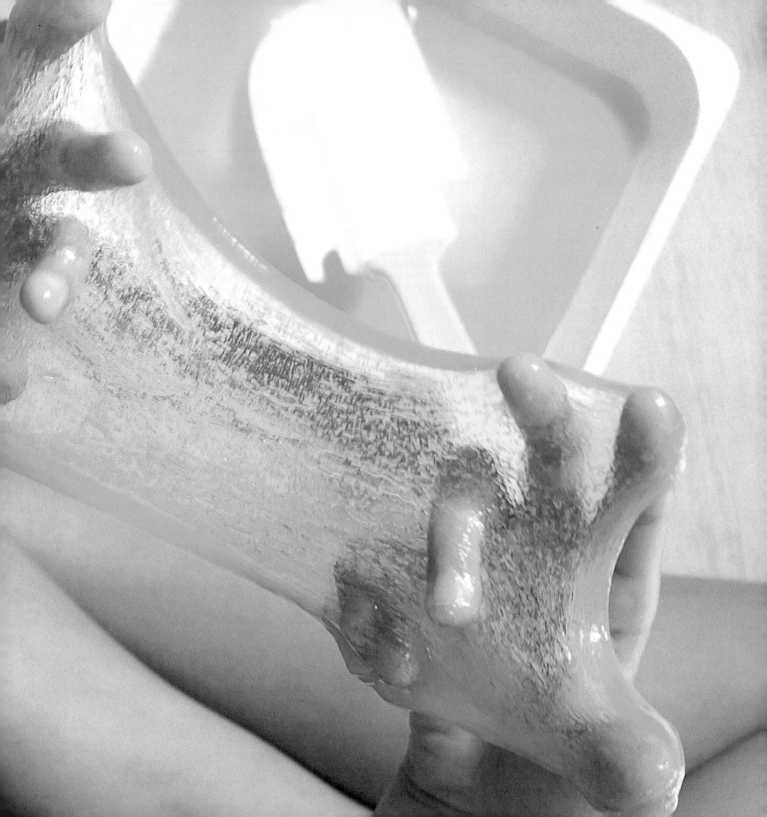

GLOW-IN-THE-DARK GOO

What You'll Need: cornstarch, a big bowl, food coloring, water, non-toxic glow-in-the-dark paint

What You'll Do: Find a good place to work outdoors that's washable because this experiment is really messy! Fill up the bowl with cornstarch and add water a little bit at a time. Mix with your hands continuously, until what you see is a slimy, sticky substance. If you want to make it green or orange, use some food coloring, but be careful. Food coloring can stain your clothes and skin too!

What You'll Observe: Play with your slime you made and see what it does. Can you form it into a ball-like shape? When you throw it down onto a surface, what happens? Try placing it under a strong light and then turn out the lights. The inside of your garage might be a good place to try this part. When you turn off the lights your spooky glue should glow in the dark!

Kid playing with hand-made goo.

The Science Behind It: The slime you made is called a non-Newtonian fluid. It doesn't flow like milk or water normally do. The chemical composition of the slime is composed of molecules that are organized in long chains. When they are pulled on, the liquid flows. However, when you push them together, they form a solid by sticking.

Things To Think About: Have you ever heard of flubber? Flubber is a non-Newtonian fluid. Have you ever played with Silly Putty? It's a non-Newtonian fluid, too. Goo is sometimes called oobleck. Can you find out why?

Eggs

THE DISAPPEARING EGG SHELL

What You'll Need: an uncooked egg, white vinegar, and a glass.

What You'll Do: Place the egg into the glass and completely cover it with vinegar. Leave it undisturbed for 4 or 5 days. Go check it out and see what happened.

What You'll Observe: After the egg is submerged under the vinegar for a while you should notice some little bubbles that are forming around the shell. This is a clue that a chemical reaction is happening. Eventually, you'll notice that there's some leftover shell in the vinegar but the yolk and egg should be floating there.

Eggs in a Glass Bowl.

The Science Behind It: The acid from the vinegar dissolves the eggshell, which is basically calcium carbonate. The inside of the egg will still be whole because the vinegar doesn't dissolve it. Some of the liquid seeps into the egg so the egg swells up a bit.

Things To Think About: What do you think would happen if you substituted a boiled egg for the raw egg in this experiment? Try it and find out!

French vanilla meringue cookies.

MAKING MERINGUE

What You'll Need: A bowl, an electric mixer, three eggs, six tablespoons of white granulated sugar, a baking sheet, and some parchment paper.

What You'll Do: Use parchment paper to line a baking sheet. Preheat your oven to 140 degrees Fahrenheit. Separate the eggs and put the egg whites into a bowl. Keep the egg yolks in the refrigerator for another use. Turn your electric mixer on low and beat the egg whites until you notice that they are starting to expand.

When you lift the beaters of the electric mixer out, the whites should be starting to stick a little bit. Now start to add the sugar slowly a tablespoon or so each time and keep beating until the sugar is all dissolved in the egg whites. The meringue will now have stiff peaks. Make *"cookies"* by plopping a couple of tablespoons of mixture on the parchment paper for each one.

Whipped egg white.

Separate your blobs of meringue by a few inches. When you're finished using up all the unbaked meringue, place it in the oven on the lower shelf for about 45 minutes. Then turn the oven off, but leave them in for another 15 or 20 minutes.

Meringue isolated on white background.

What You'll Observe: The egg whites started to expand as you beat air into them. They got stiff and became even stiffer after the sugar was added.

The Science Behind It: When you beat the egg whites, it unfolds their protein molecules. As you continue to beat, you're trapping bubbles of air into these protein molecules and it transforms it into a foam. The addition of sugar makes the egg whites even stiffer. When baked, the meringues harden into crunchy goodness.

Macaroon is sweet meringue-based confection.

Things To Think About: There's a lot of science going on in your kitchen every day. Now it's time to put out some Strawberries, Ice Cream, and a Meringue cookie or two to eat!

Awesome! Now you know more about how to do some simple experiments with food and kitchen ingredients. You can find more Science and Nature books from Baby Professor by searching the website of your favorite book retailer.

Made in the USA
Middletown, DE
08 September 2020